Everything Elvis

Everything Elvis

Joni Mabe

THUNDER'S
MOUTH
PRESS

First Thunder's Mouth Press Edition, 1996

Published by
Thunder's Mouth Press
632 Broadway, Seventh Floor,
New York, NY 10012

The publisher would like to thank Angelo Hornak for his contribution to this book, beyond the
call of duty.

Joni Mabe's Traveling Panoramic Encyclopedia of Everything Elvis
is not affiliated with Elvis Presley Estates.

Designed by Wherefore Art?

Library of Congress Cataloging in Publication Data

Mabe . Joni Lee , 1957–
    Everything Elvis / Joni Mabe.
        p.   cm.
    Features over 100 reproductions of objects from Mabe's "Traveling
Panoramic Encyclopedia of Everything Elvis,"   including textured
collages of images of Elvis Presley.
    Includes index.
    ISBN 1-56025-107-7
    1. Presley, Elvis. 1935-1977--Portraits. 2. Presley, Elvis,
1935-1977--Collectibles---Pictorial works.   1. Title.   96-24702
ML420.P96M25   1996   CIP
782.42166 092--dc20   MN

Printed and bound by Imago Publishing in Singapore

2 4 6 8 10 9 7 5 3 1

Distributed by
Publishers Group West
4065 Hollis Street
Emeryville, CA 94608

Introduction

The whole Elvis experience has been a roller-coaster ride that shows no sign of stopping. For a whole epoch in US history Elvis has been a touchstone, as essential a figure as the post-World War Two world has produced. Elvis became the main man, the one link in the chain you had to define yourself against if you were to make sense of your place in the on-going and inescapable drama of pop culture.

My own life can be divided into two halves: pre-EDD and post-EDD - EDD meaning Elvis Death Day. The first twenty years of my life were spent oblivious of the King. He was too familiar, too obvious a piece of our cultural landscape, a seeming relic to my youthful mind intent on newer and more immediate pleasures to be found in Hendrix, Led Zepplin, Lynyrd Skynyrd, Waylon Jennings, Aretha Franklin, and the Allman Brothers. Elvis was a legend, but one so firmly wrapped in his Elvis shroud that many of us failed to recognize that there was infinitely more there than Colonel Parker would care for us to see.

My indifference to Elvis came to an end on 16 August 1977. On that hot summer day, I was washing and waxing my beloved 1964 International Scout when the news broke on the radio. I was stunned: the perfection of the image (in his earlier years) and the thought of that creature's earthly death dealt me a greater blow than I could have ever imagined. Elvis may not have invented rock 'n' roll, but it is surely his ascent that brought the music home to greater America. I was grateful to the radio for going on an Elvis binge that day and I discovered the range of music he performed. He seemed to absorb it all - good and bad - and give to each song

Joni holding the infamous Elvis Wart preserved in formaldehyde.

exactly what was required. That day became a day of grief and rejoicing for me: irreparable loss and fabulous discovery all at once. My newfound feelings were further strengthened by the incomprehension and indifference of the media centers to Elvis's death. That night, as I recall, ABC's *Nightline* gave a rather listless report on Elvis's departure. I remember Ted Koppel asking some poor college professor what the big deal was about this particular singer. Koppel wanted to reduce the whole issue to the question of technical ability - no need to delve into what cannot be fitted into an already existing set of categories. Elvis's arrival was to a large extent about the explosion of such categories. Elvis became a powerful and complex image of freedom.

The art world as I knew it around 1980 was unbendingly dedicated to what was serious, political and obscure. It was my ambition to ignore those barriers and strike out for territory where various audiences outside the art world could explore my vision. Elvis became the vehicle through which I played out my notions about America, the South, sex, religion, death and whatever else took my fancy. The idea of an Elvis museum grew out of the sheer accumulation of Elvis objects alongside my own original artworks.

After years of showing my Elvis collection to friends and visitors in my home, I installed the first 'Elvis Room' in a public gallery in 1983. From that time on, the museum grew as well as the title, which several years later became known as 'Joni Mabe's Traveling Panoramic Encyclopedia of Everything Elvis'. The entire museum has played to audiences across the USA and even Britain. Works from the museum have been shown across the globe.

My glitter magnets are called 'Elvis Mosaics', in tribute to my confidence that the subject and execution are worthy of their Renaissance predecessors. When these works are installed in a gallery space with thousands of other Elvis-related objects all systematically arranged, the overall atmosphere is that of a pop cathedral. And since it has been on continuous tour for twelve years, I believe P.T. Barnum himself would be proud.

Two items in the museum which excite special interest and delight, equivalent to Barnum's Fiji Mermaid and Jumbo the Elephant, are the *Maybe Elvis Toenail* and the *Elvis Wart*. The toenail I found in the Jungle Room at Graceland during my first pilgrimage to the newly opened estate. The year was 1983 and I was scouring the premises for signs that the King had really lived there. That is when I stumbled on this toenail embedded in the carpet. I cannot guarantee that the nail hails from the King's toe, but who else would be taking such liberties as clipping their nails in the Jungle Room? The wart I bought from a doctor in Memphis who removed it from Elvis's right wrist in 1958. It is clear from photographs that he tried to hide it but finally rid himself of the bothersome wart.

Showing the collection has indeed been an amazing period of mine and Elvis's life. His afterlife has been more eventful and strange than any afterlife has a right to be. For me, immersion in his image and music, multiple treks to Graceland, and steady touring of the museum have brought me closer to Elvis's meaning and power than any mere analysis could have done. But it has been the response of people to my museum that has insured its success. The range of feeling has alternated between outright hostility and an almost rapturous recognition of shared obsession. It's been a hoot.

This obsession gave me a subject that has been a big part of my work and it seems he is even a part of my immediate family. My life has been dedicated to preserving his memory. It is easy to love a dead man who lives in my dreams.

9

Joni Mabe
Athens, Georgia
May 1996

16 August 1983

Dear Elvis,

You don't know how many times
I've dreamt and wished that
you were my lover - or father.
But you died without a trace of
myself ever touching your life. I
could have saved you, Elvis. We
could have found happiness together at
Graceland. I know that I could have put
your broken self back together. It's as
if you could have discovered that sex and
religion could be brought together in
your feelings for me.

The hurt you carried every day, the
passion that dried up with the years, I
could have restored. All of those women
sapped your spirit and gave you nothing
but the simulation of passion. I know the
secrets of the Southern night.

I worship you. My sleep is filled with
longing for you. I try to make a go of
daily life but all else fades before this
consuming image of yourself always
present in my mind. This image guides me
to the places I want to be. I lie here
now thinking, agonizing - in other words
masturbating over the impossibility of

10

ever being your slave.
Sometimes I feel I've
been hypnotized, that I
can no longer bear
existence without you.
Other men in their
fleshly selves could never
measure up to your
perfection. When making
love to you in the later
years, I still could sense
your throbbing manliness. You
really touched the woman in me.
I no longer know the difference between
fact and fantasy. My poisoned spirit
cries out for relief, for just one caress
to remind me that you really were a man
and not a god. If God listened to my
prayers you'd be lying beside me now.

No matter who I'm with, it's always you.
Elvis, I have a confession to make: I'm
        carrying your child. The last
        Elvis imitator I humped was
        carrying your sacred seed.
        Please send money. Enclosed
        are the photographs of
        myself and the earthly
        messenger you sent.

        Love-sick for you, Baby ...

    Joni

The **Love Me Tender**, **Sincerely Elvis** *frame was manufactured in 1956 by Elvis Presley Enterprises.*

Big El.

13

I made each one of these unique prints entitled **Big El** *in the early 1980s.*
They are lithographs adorned with glitter, sequins and lace.

14

The Official
Elvis
Prayer Rug, *1988,*
has brought good
luck and fortune to
thousands of people.

Your instructions on how to use

THE OFFICIAL ELVIS PRAYER RUG

1. Take rug into bathroom, late at night when everyone is sleeping.
2. Lay rug on the floor, with Elvis side up.
3. Look into Elvis's eyes.
4. Kneel before the rug and touch the bottom of the rug with both knees. It must touch both knees.
5. Ask Elvis anything you need from the following list. Please check only one. Only one prayer can be answered with one rug.

15

☐ I need healing for ☐ high ☐ low blood pressure.

☐ I need healing for a problem with my back.

☐ I have stiffness and pain because of arthritis.

☐ I need more than one thousand dollars.

☐ I want you to pray about past due financial obligations.

6. Do this for forty days, and forty nights, then send Joni $40.00, and your prayers will be answered.
7. Pass along your Elvis Prayer Rug to another lost soul and buy another one for yourself.

Act now before it's too late.

LIMITED NUMBER OF RUGS AVAILABLE.

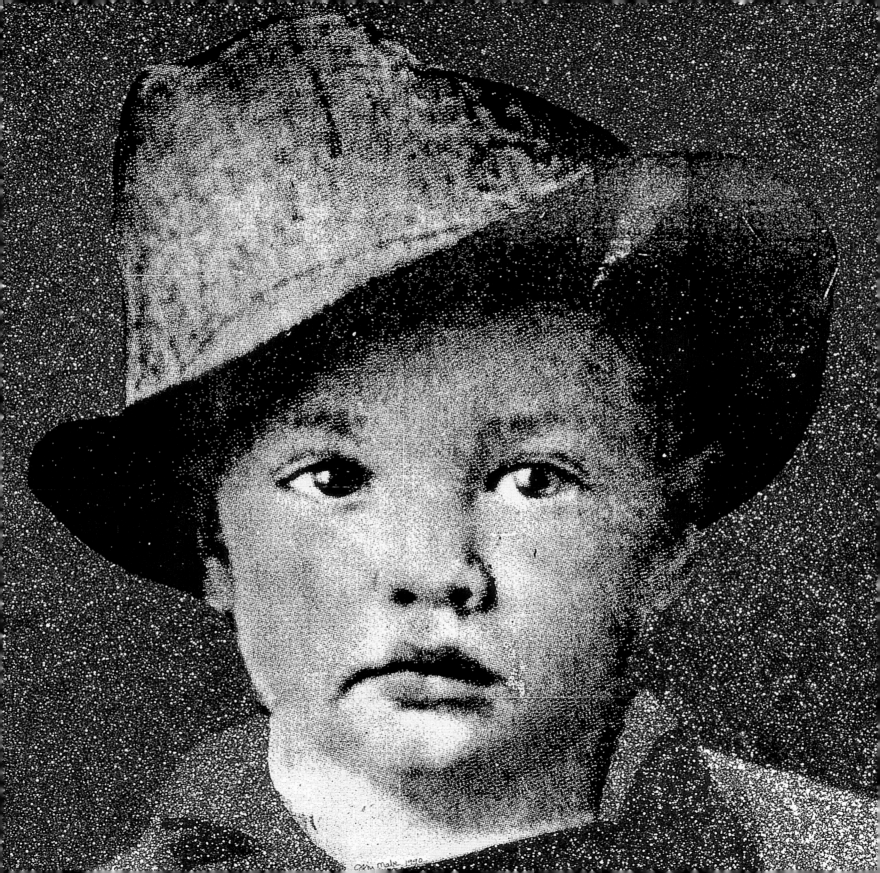

The Maybe *Elvis Toenail* I found in the green shag carpet in the Jungle Room at Graceland during my first visit in *1983*.

18

It was embedded in one of the shag fibers near the sofa. I wasn't looking for **Elvis's toenail** clipping - I just wanted to touch where **Elvis** had walked.

Opposite: Water from **Elvis's** swimming pool.

ELVIS' WART MAGNIFIED 10,000 TIMES.

JONI MABE 1992

Whenever I travel to install the Traveling Panoramic Encyclopedia of Everything Elvis, the wart and toenail always travel with me on the plane instead of being shipped inside the crates, because they are priceless and there won't be any more.

The *Elvis Wart* I bought from a doctor in Memphis, Tennessee, in *1990*.

Elvis had it removed in **1958**. Why the doctor kept it all these years I don't know. Maybe he knew something we don't.

The wart is as big as a black-eyed pea.

I organized the Elvis Wart Tour '94 and took the wart along with my Traveling Panoramic Encyclopedia of Everything Elvis to London. I figured since Elvis never got to tour Britain while he was alive, I would take the wart sightseeing. In London, we went to the top of St Paul's Cathedral, Westminster Abbey, and Buckingham Palace; then we rented a car and toured Stonehenge, Brighton beach, and Cornwall, and even traveled to Fishguard, Wales.

Elvis ornaments I made for Christmas.
Every holiday can be an Elvis occasion.

Love Me Tender, *1989.*

The King's death made it difficult for us to be together.

However in dreamland I assume the form of Ann Margaret
and we carry on beyond the last frames of Viva La Vegas.

Hawaii

G.

Fun in
Acapulco

Lou

Change
of Habit

Ro

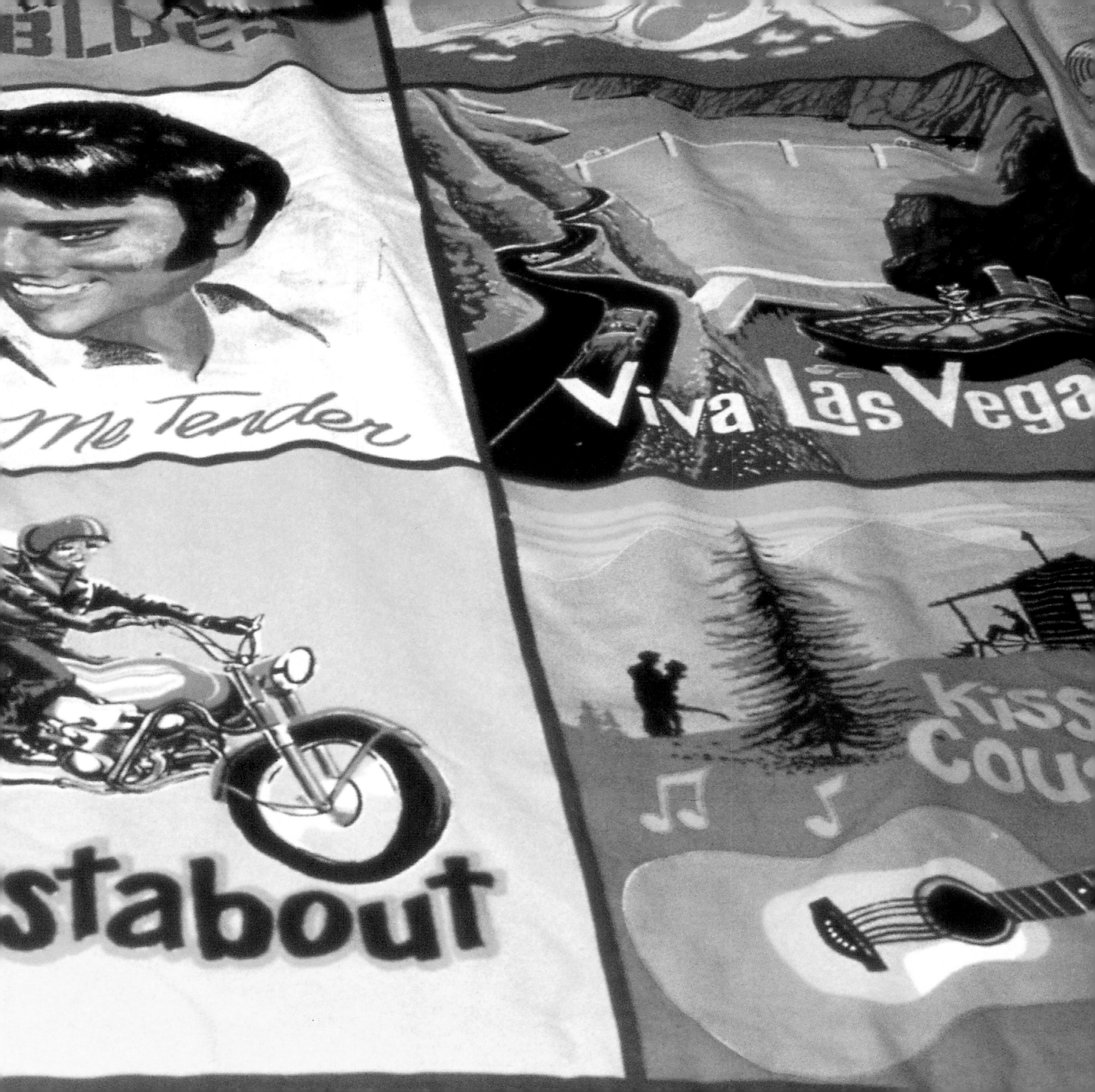
Me Tender
Viva Las Vega
stabout

Hound Dog, *1989.*

Jailhouse Rock, *1989*.

30

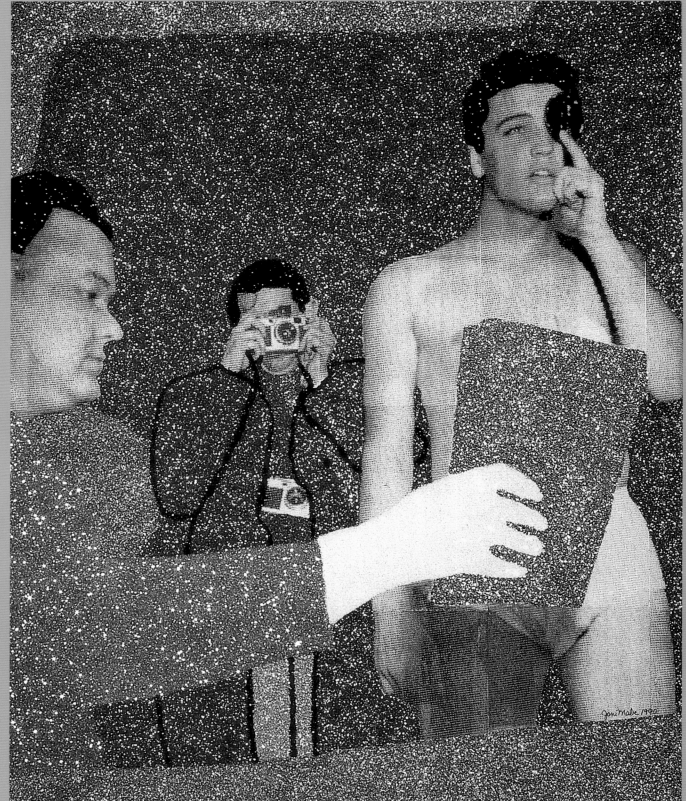

Elvis Eye Test
*during his
induction into
the army in
1958*

ELVIS AND VERNON JOIN THE CONFEDERACY

31

When I hear Elvis sing the 'American Trilogy' I envision Elvis and Vernon fighting for the Confederacy. If Elvis had been born in 1835 instead of 1935 he would have served in the Confederate States Army during the War Between the States. And since he was such a mama's boy, Gladys would have sent Vernon along to look after her boy.

It took two weeks to make the *Elvis Button Coat,* 1990.

It has approximately 3000 buttons that I made with my button maker and weighs about 30 pounds.
I have worn it on special occasions, such as the Candlelight Service on the eve of the anniversary of Elvis's death
and to openings, but it is so heavy that when the night is over I am about four inches shorter.

34

The *Elvis Button Dress,* 1988.

Over 1000 buttons/badges.

36

The *Elvis Button Jacket,* 1983.

Approximately 450 buttons.

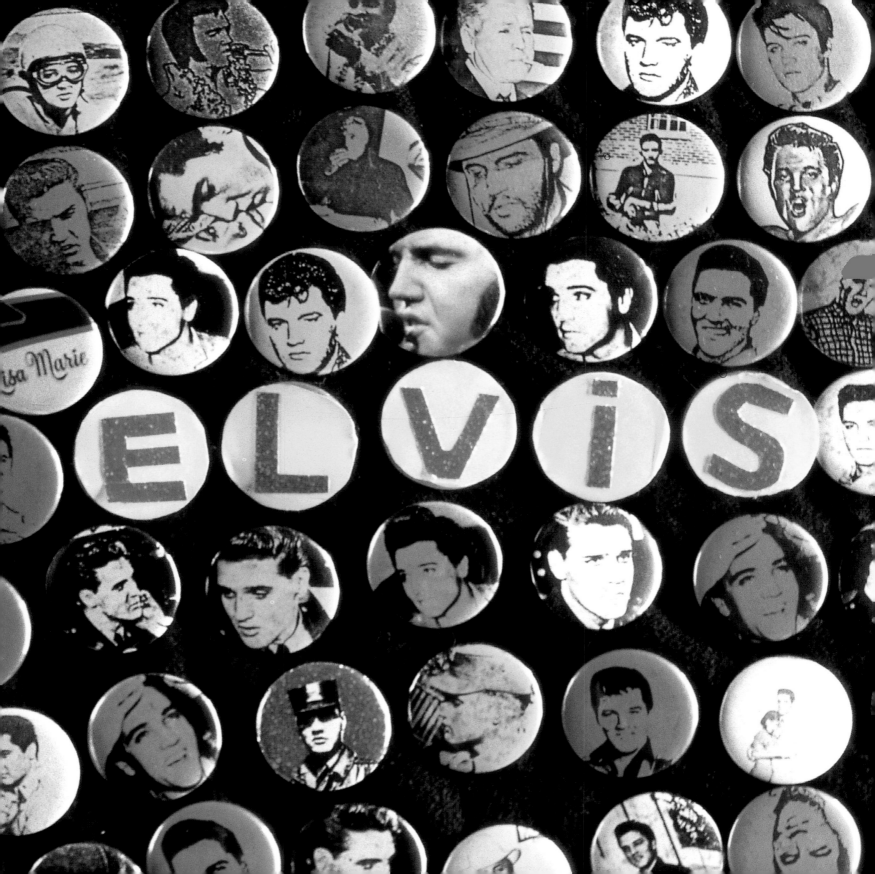

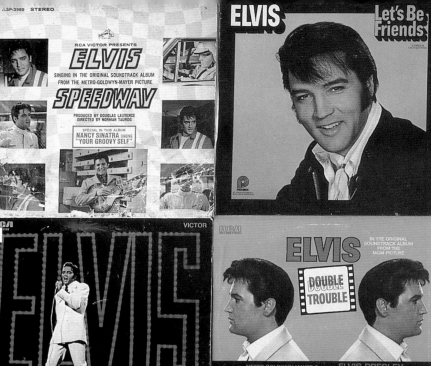

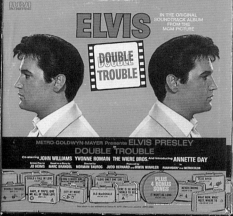

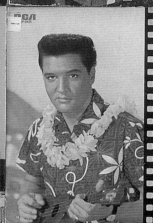

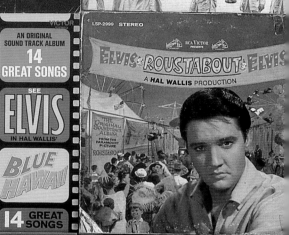

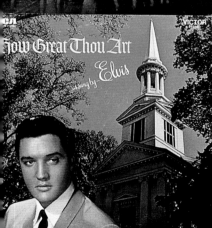

THE ELVIS PRESLEY

ALBUM OF JUKE BOX FAVORITES

CONTENTS

BLUE SUEDE SHOES

I WAS THE ONE

TENNESSEE SATURDAY NIGHT

MY BABY LEFT ME

I'M LEFT, YOU'RE RIGHT, SHE'S GONE

Dynamic Star of
Television, Records,
Radio and Movies

ABERBACH (LONDON) LTD.

Price **2/6**

42

This is a page spread from **The Elvis Presley Scrapbook**, *Volume 2, that I created in*

1982.

I focused on Elvis during the 1950s, collected images from magazines during that time period and put Elvis in different environments and situations. There are four of these books in the edition, each one unique.

43

Elvis needed a strong woman who understood his Southern ways.

I COULD HAVE SAVED ELVIS ONLY if I HAD BEEN DORN EARLIER....

by JONI MABE

DORN 1957

Hillbilly Cat Wood Plaque *and* **Elvis Wood Plaque**
are collages made of walnut wood.

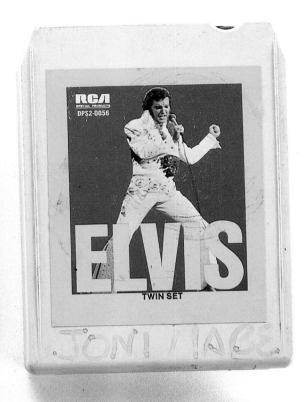

46

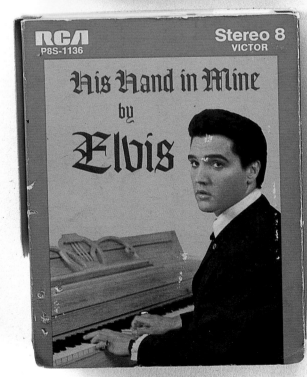

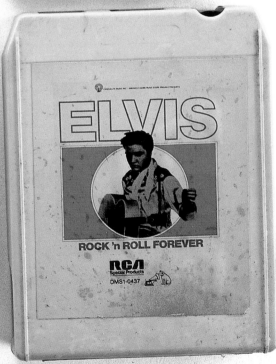

Authentic
Elvis fan dress
from the 1950s.

49

Elvis Shopping Bag, *1991.*

Elvis Valentine Hearts,

above 1984 and opposite 1989.

THE
ELVIS PRESLEY
SCRAPBOOK
by
JONI MABE

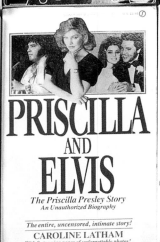
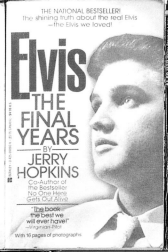
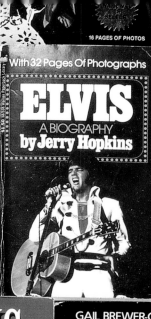
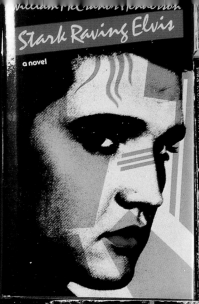

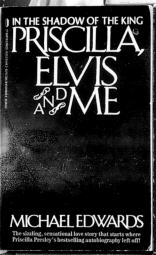
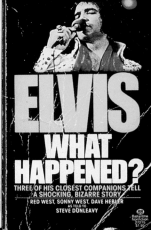
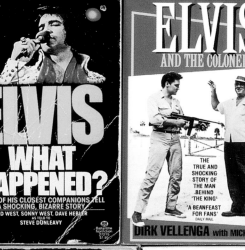

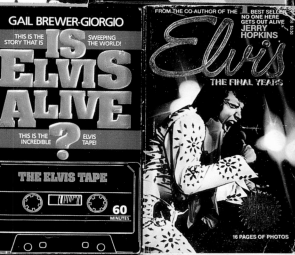

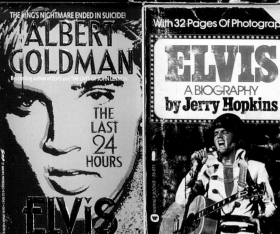
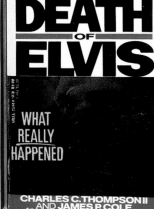

58

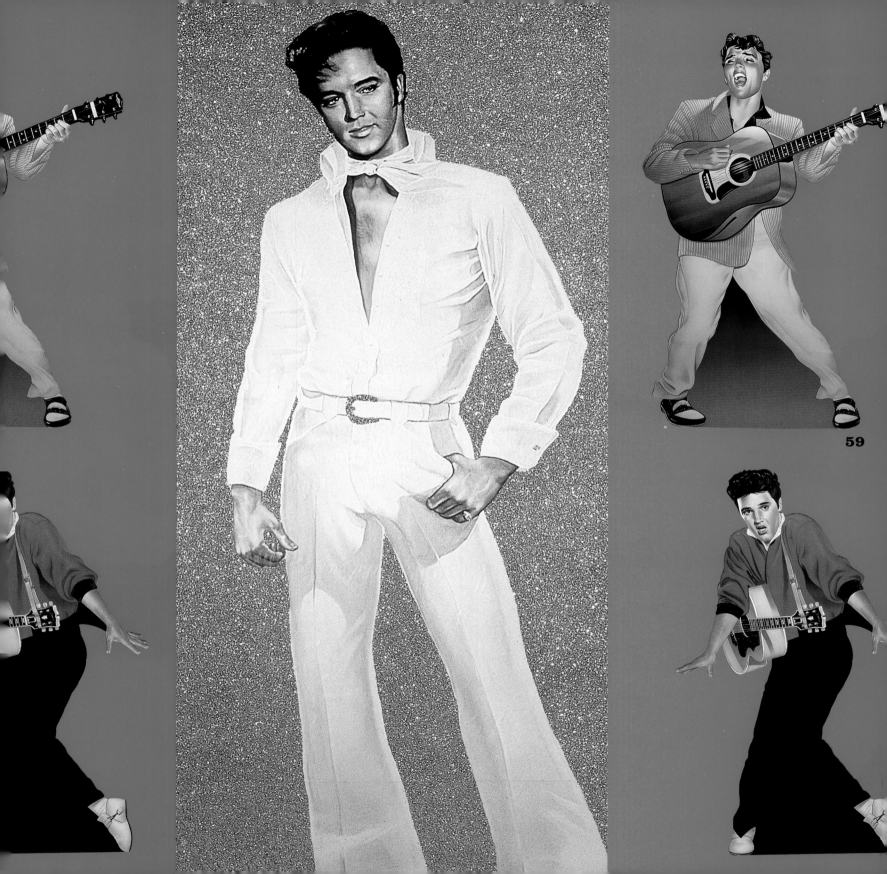

59

Elvis Mosaics.

Afro Sheen Elvis, *1983, shows Elvis giving his sexy 'I don't give a damn' look.*

ELVIS PRESLEY
1935-1977

64

29 USA

ROCK & ROLL SINGER, 1935-1977

ELVIS

FIRST DAY OF ISSUE

January 8, 1993 • Memphis, TN 38101

65

Elvis Presley

Trading shark-skin suit for olive-drab uniform,
serving his country at home and abroad.

DNA SCIENTISTS TO DIG UP ELVIS!

Tissue samples will settle the mystery of the century . . . . IS IT REALLY PRESLEY'S CORPSE IN THE COFFIN?

74

Elvis
Mosaics

Elvis Mosaics.

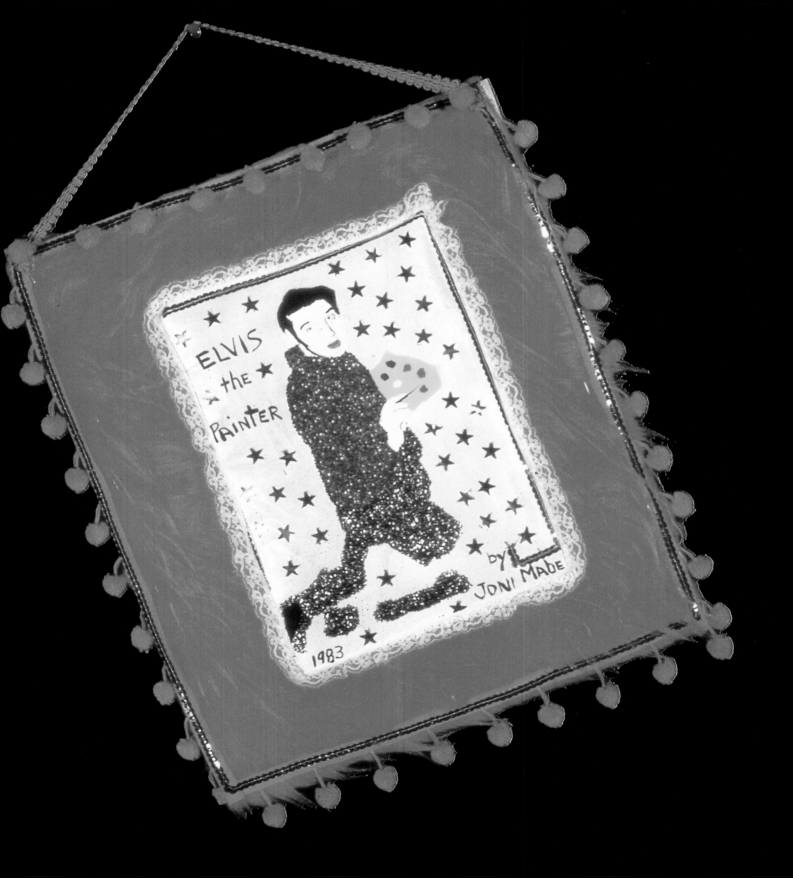

Swamp Thang Elvis, *1989*, is a color Xerox transfer with actual human hair, glitter and fringe border.

The Elvis Presley Scrapbook, *Volume 2,* *1982.*

ELVIS TOURS CENTRAL AMERICA, BRINGS HOPE TO HOPELESS, FOOD TO THE HUNGRY. BY JONI MABE 84

84

When I first became an
Elvis fan I worshipped
the young Elvis - the
1956 King - but as the
years have flown by I
have found the Vegas
Elvis to be an object of
great fascination.

85

Sincerely,
Elvis Presley

86

I bought this Elvis plaster relief bust in Hartford, Connecticut, in 1981.
Everywhere I go I search for more Elvis objects

*This **Gold Lamé Jacket** replica I created in 1990 for Elvis impersonators to wear while they perform.*

90

HAPPY BIRTHDAY

BABY ELVIS

(JESSE TOO)

I don't think Elvis ever recovered from the fact that his twin brother, Jesse, died at birth and he lived.

If Elvis were alive in 1991 at the age of fifty-six, he would have to be incognito. But I believe he is dead.

Shrine for Elvis Hair, *1989.*
I bought some of Elvis's hair from a woman in Los Angeles who knew Elvis's hairdresser, Larry Geller.

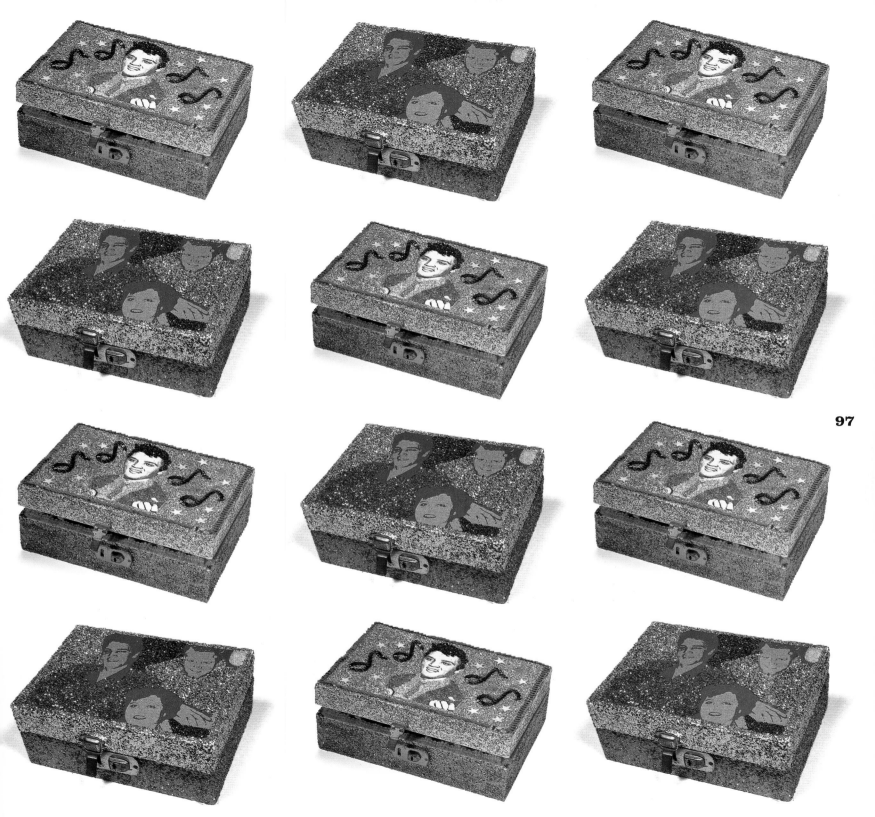

Elvis Jewelry Boxes, *1983 and 1990.*

Elvis Customized
Moody Blue
Dress.

98

I made this dress in 1985 and have worn it on many occasions.

DNA SCIENTISTS TO DIG UP ELVIS!

WEEKLY WORLD NEWS

August 22, 1995 99¢/$1.09 CANADA 70p U.K.

104

Tissue samples will settle the mystery of the century . . . *IS IT REALLY PRESLEY'S CORPSE IN THE COFFIN?*

Presley phones President to announce comeback concert!

ELVIS COMING OUT OF HIDING ON FEB. 25!

105

60-yr.-old Presley talks with Clinton!

Voice analysis of White House tape proves The King really did fake his death in 1977!

0 74851 08101 3

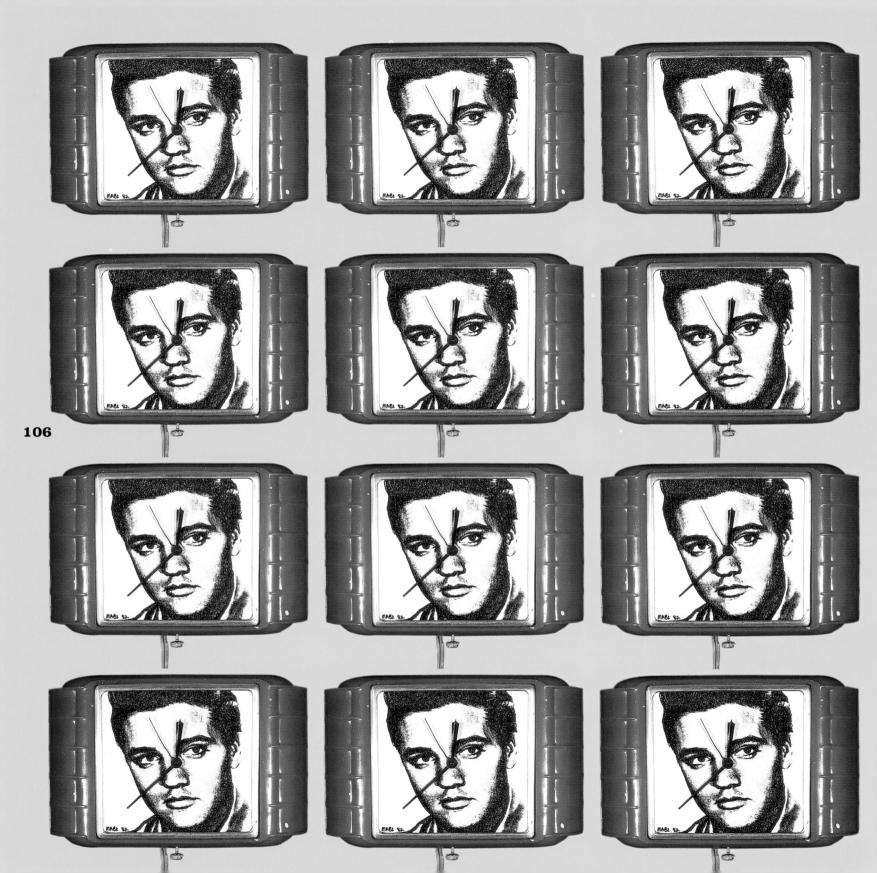

106

Elvis Car Tire Shrine, *1996.*

108

I created
Mr Wiggle
in 1983

109

during the most
desperate phase of
my Elvis obsession.

Life After Life

17 August 1977: President Jimmy Carter states that 'Elvis Presley's death deprives our country of a part of itself. He was unique and irreplaceable... His music and his personality... permanently changed the face of American popular culture.'

17 August 1977: Elvis Presley's interest-free checking account balance at the time of his death is $1,055,000. 69.

18 August 1977: The Reverend G.W. Bradley of the Woodvale Church of Christ in Memphis officiates at a private funeral service at Graceland and in his address tells mourners that Elvis Presley 'dared to be different.'

18 August 1977: Governor Raymond Blanton of Tennessee orders that all state flags should be flown at half-mast to mark an official day of mourning in the state.

18 August 1977: A motorcade said to be of either eleven or fourteen white- and cream-colored Cadillacs, flanked by motorcycle outriders, accompanies the white Cadillac hearse from Graceland to Forest Hill Cemetery, Memphis.

18 August 1977: Elvis's close friend Liberace sends to Graceland an enormous floral arrangement in the shape of a guitar.

112

21 August 1977: RCA reports that it has sold over eight million Elvis Presley records in the six days since his death.

6 September 1977: A photograph, allegedly of Elvis Presley lying in his coffin, appears on the cover of **The National Enquirer**, which then sells a record six and a half million copies.

13 September 1977: Fans march on Washington in a campaign to persuade the Federal government to mark an official Elvis Presley Day. Maryland Congresswoman Barbara Mikulski introduces a bill in Congress to make 8 January a national holiday but she receives insufficient support.

September 1977: 'The King is Gone' by Ronnie McDowell climbs to No. 13 in the Billboard chart.

2 October 1977: The bodies of Elvis and his mother Gladys Presley are moved from the Forest Hill Cemetery and reburied side by side in a patch of Graceland which Elvis named 'the Meditation Garden' (right). A memorial flame is lit which reads: 'May this flame reflect our never-ending respect and love for you. May it serve as a constant reminder to each of us of your eternal presence.'

Left: Elvis Presley's grave on what would have been his sixtieth birthday.

3 October 1977: CBS broadcasts **Elvis In Concert**, a one-hour special recorded four months earlier in which Elvis sings numbers including **'Also Sprach Zarathustra,' 'My Way'** and **'Jailhouse Rock.'**

27 November 1977: The Meditation Garden at Graceland is opened to the public.

28 November 1977: **Elvis** by Ray Cooney and Jack Good opens at the Astoria Theatre in London with Tim Whitnall, Shakin' Stevens and James (P.J.) Proby playing Elvis from boyhood to middle age.

8 January 1978: NBC screens a ninety-minute special **Nashville Remembers Elvis On His Birthday** with appearances by, amongst others, Jerry Lee Lewis, Merle Haggard and Carl Perkins.

1 February 1978: Elvis is inducted into **Playboy** magazine's 'Musical Hall of Fame.'

1 June 1978: Elmer and Debra Flint are the first couple to be married inside Elvis's birthplace in Old Saltillo Road, East Tupelo, Mississippi.

114

1 September 1978: The first annual Elvis Presley Convention opens at the Hilton Hotel in Las Vegas - the first time that there is a gathering of Elvis impersonators and that the best Elvis impersonator of the year is chosen.

Above: Elvis impersonators.

8 September 1978: The Las Vegas Hilton unveils a 400-lb, six-foot bronze statue of Elvis, made for $150,000 by Carl Romanelli and with a memorial which reads: 'Memories of Elvis Presley will always be with us.'

Right: Elvis statue, London.

The truth
will rock you

Elvis

THE MO

A John Carpenter Film
Starring KURT RUSSELL as Elvis

Laurence Myers Presents **ELVIS THE MOVIE** A Dick Clark Production
Starring KURT RUSSELL as Elvis Presley · SHELLEY WINTERS as Gladys Presley · BING RUSSELL as Vernon Presley
ROBERT GRAY as Red West · SEASON HUBLEY as Priscilla Presley · PAT HINGLE as Colonel Tom Parker · ABI YOUNG as Nata
CHARLIE HODGE as Himself · PELICIA FENSKE as Lisa Marie Presley · RANDY GRAY as Elvis, as a Boy
Executive Producer DICK CLARK   Producer/Writer ANTHONY LAWRENCE   Director JOHN CARPENTER   Director of Photography DONALD M. MOR
Music Composed and Conducted By JOE RENZETTI   Elvis Vocals Sung By RONNIE McDOWELL
Soundtrack Album available on Arcade Records
Distributed by GTO FILMS CERTIFICATE 'U'

18 October 1978: *The Gong Show* on NBC is devoted entirely to a line-up of Elvis impersonators.

1 December 1978: Psychic David Behr claims to have made contact with Elvis and to have asked him a total of sixty-five questions. Recordings of the conversation go on sale for $9.95.

18 December 1978: Impersonator Herbert Baer of Manitowoc, Wisconsin, changes his name to Elvis Presley.

8 January 1979: The foundations are laid in Elvis Presley Park, Tupelo, Mississippi, for the Elvis Presley Chapel. Supporters of the project claim that it was Elvis himself who suggested that building a chapel in God's name was the best way to remember him.

11 February 1979: ABC airs **Elvis**, a three-hour TV movie starring Kurt Russell as Elvis and Shelley Winters as his mother and direction by John Carpenter. It attracts a Nielsen rating of 27-3, beating both **Gone With the Wind** and **One Flew Over the Cuckoo's Nest** in audience figures.

Opposite page: Graceland, 1987

13 August 1985: *Are You Lonesome Tonight?*, the play by Alan Bleasdale, opens at London's Phoenix Theatre with Martin Shaw as Elvis and Simon Bowman as his younger self.

February 1986: Elvis is posthumously inducted into the Rock and Roll Hall of Fame in Cleveland, Ohio, in the company of such notables as Chuck Berry, Little Richard and Ray Charles.

22 September 1986: *The Twilight Zone* features an episode called **'The Once and Future King,'** about a Presley impersonator who mistakenly kills the real singer.

1987: Elvis Presley Enterprises offers **Elvis: the Game That Allows the Legend to Live On.**

July 1987: In London **The Independent** newspaper reports that a Bristol man has insured his collection of Elvis memorabilia for £20,000 and has acquired a rattlesnake to guard the treasures.

August 1987: RCA announce that they took orders for ten million Elvis Presley albums in the twenty-four hours following the tenth anniversary of his death.

August 1987: The short-lived Manchester newspaper **News on Sunday** features Peter 'Elvis' Singh, the Rocking Sikh, who, with his band, the Screaming Pakistanis, perform such well-loved songs as **'Turbans Over Memphis,'** **'Bhindi Bhaji Boogie'** and **'Back in the Golden Temple of Amritsar.'**

August 1987: **USA Today** conducts a telephone poll to establish which Elvis song is Top of the Pops among his fans. **'Suspicious Minds'** comes first with 31 per cent, followed by **'Love Me Tender'** at 24 per cent.

Summer 1987: Lucy de Barbin with Dary Matera writes a book entitled *Are You Lonesome Tonight? The Untold Story of Elvis Presley's One True Love - and the Child He Never Knew.*

October 1987: Louise Welling, a Kalamazoo woman, claims to have made two sightings of Elvis, three weeks apart, in Vicksburg - firstly in a grocery store and then in a Burger King restaurant. After the story breaks, a local diner offers Don't Be Cruel Gruel and a dentist in the area advertises with the slogan 'The King gets regular check-ups here.'

1988: Every Elvis fan will want the first Delphi Elvis Presley collectors' plate. The first of them is 'Elvis at the Gates of Graceland' and there will be eight different series of as many as sixteen different plates.

5 January 1985: London's Hammersmith Palais holds what would have been Elvis Presley's 50th birthday party.

8 January 1985: Priscilla Presley hosts the first televised tour of Graceland.

8 January 1985: The British Post Office celebrates with a special Elvis Presley stamp and first-day cover.

August 1985: Paul Simon records the album **Graceland** in honor of Elvis. It receives several Grammy awards.

January 1988: It is reported that Elvis Presley is the biggest posthumous money-earner, followed by John Lennon, Jimi Hendrix and Jim Morrison.

7 and 8 February 1988: ABC airs **Elvis and Me** (right), a two-part two-hour mini-series based on Priscilla Presley's account of her relationship with Elvis. It attracts an audience of more than sixty-three million viewers and becomes the highest-rated TV movie of the 1987-88 season.

24 April 1988: The **People** reports that a nightwatchman at an Elvis Presley exhibition in London hands in his notice after finding the candle at the shrine mysteriously lit and the door of the Cadillac wide open.

17 September 1988: American Express issues an Elvis Presley mastercard.

20 September 1988: The U.S. **Sun** reports that a Soviet space probe has seen a statue of Elvis on Mars and that the statue beamed 'All Shook Up' in the probe's direction.

September 1988: It is reported that more than eight thousand people have asked to see the photograph of Elvis meeting Richard Nixon of 1970 - by far the most popular exhibit this summer in the National Archives in Washington.

4 October 1988: The National Enquirer's cover story is entitled 'Elvis Is Alive,' with photographs taken the previous month allegedly of Elvis.

October 1988: It is reported that Elvis Presley has been sighted in Hawaii. It seems that he has lost his hair and that he has taken to wearing a muu-muu, a dress worn by Hawaiian women.

27 November 1988: The **Mail on Sunday** reveals that Waco waitress Candy La Flaire is convinced that her $10 Presley ceramic table lamp serenades her every night with 'Hound Dog' and 'Love Me Tender.'

29 December 1988: It is reported that Raisa Gorbachev has helped to arrange the Moscow staging of the show **Forever Elvis**, breaking a ban on the music of Elvis Presley in the Soviet Union that had lasted thirty years.

8 January 1989: El Vez, the Mexican Elvis interpreter, makes his debut in Hollywood, California.

14 February 1989: The **Sun** holds a readers' poll to find out how many people believe that Elvis is still alive.

15 February 1989: Bookmakers William Hill slash odds to 250-1 that Elvis will be found alive within the next year.

Right: American Express credit card sold at auction in 1994.

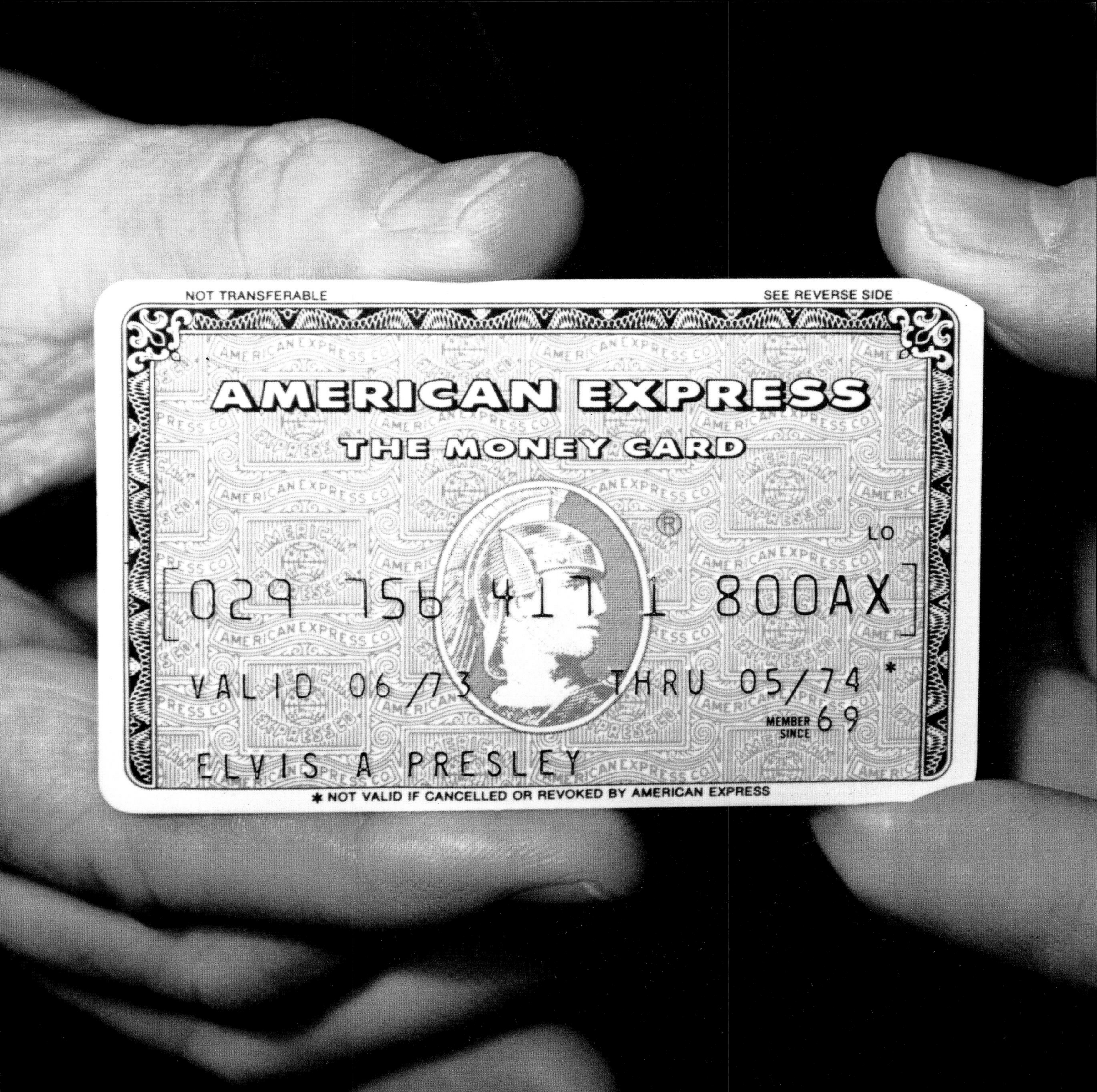
NOT TRANSFERABLE
SEE REVERSE SIDE
AMERICAN EXPRESS
THE MONEY CARD
LO
029 756 417 1 800AX
VALID 06/73 THRU 05/74 *
MEMBER SINCE 69
ELVIS A PRESLEY
* NOT VALID IF CANCELLED OR REVOKED BY AMERICAN EXPRESS

15 February 1989: *The Sun* issues a challenge. It will pay one million pounds to anybody producing the real Elvis at the newspaper's headquarters at Wapping, east London. Presley will have to make a convincing attempt at **'All Shook Up,' 'Blue Suede Shoes'** and **'Hound Dog,'** and furnish a good explanation of what he's been doing since August 1977.

16 February 1989: A man in Largs in Scotland offers to sell one of his kidneys for £20,000 so that he can fund his ailing wife's trip to Graceland.

29 May 1989: Elvis's daughter Lisa Marie gives birth to a baby girl named Danielle by her husband Danny Keough.

24 October 1989: *The Sun* reports that entertainer Noel Botham has released an album entitled *The Songs That Elvis Would Have Sung*.

19 November 1989: *The Mail on Sunday* profiles Danny Uwnawich of Northridge in the San Fernando Valley who has rec reated Graceland, including a replica of the gates, in a building he calls Melodyland.

May 1990: At the inaugural Elvis Presley Awards in New York, Keith Richards of the Rolling Stones presents Eric Clapton with the award for the Best Rock Guitarist.

August 1990: The Elvis Intergalactic Weight Tables are published in the US. They purport to show that Elvis would have weighted 450 stones on the Sun but a mere 13 pounds on Pluto.

10 August 1990: Russian Elvis impersonator Rafik Koshapov meets the press in St Petersburg. He cannot speak a word of English but manages to learn the songs phonetically.

17 September 1990: *The Sun* reports that Kent police inspector Neil Duncan, with his wife Jan backing him as one half of the Sweet Perspirations, will perform his Elvis impersonation act on the stage of the London Palladium.

1991: Hamilton Gifts Ltd produce a limited edition of Elvis musical figurines and music boxes.

8 January 1991: Iva Finkenbiner of Conway, South Carolina, marks what would have been Elvis's fifty-sixth birthday by baking a cake in the shape of a guitar and selling handmade blue suede shoes and hound dogs from her shop.

17 May 1991: *The Daily Star* reports that Essex shop assistant Kathy Aldrich is understandably amazed when her cash register plays **'Love Me Tender'** whenever she makes a sale in the hardware shop where she works. The mystery is solved when the manufacturers admit that they have used the song as a reminder to shopkeepers to follow certain security measures with the machine.

8 July 1991: Boris Yeltsin reveals that **'Are You Lonesome Tonight?'** is one of his favorites from the Elvis songbook.

10 August 1991: Paul MacLeod and his son, Elvis Aaron Presley MacLeod open their home, Graceland Too, in Holly Springs, Mississippi, to the public.

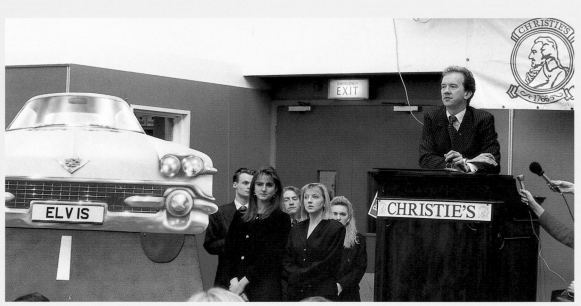

16 August 1991: Elvis impersonator Johnny Earl becomes the first man since Elvis to wear Elvis's G.I. uniform when he appears at a concert at Wembley.

19 August 1991: Elvis entrepreneur Sid Shaw is unfazed by the coup against Mikhail Gorbachev and goes ahead with his Presleystroika tour of Russia.

29 August 1991: Auctioneers Christie's of London sell a love letter which Elvis wrote to his sweetheart Anita in 1958. It sold for £4,400.

Elvis numberplate at auction at Christie's.

1992: Through the year Elvis fans can obtain three series of cards from the River Group Company which depict the singer's life and career. The complete Elvis Collection features 660 cards in colour and black and white. For Christmas, Hallmark's brass-plated Christmas ornament is bound to be on plenty of gift lists.

22 January 1992: After a two-hour special, **The Elvis Conspiracy - the Elvis Files**, is aired, a survey reveals that 70 per cent of the audience believe Elvis is still alive and in hiding.

April 1992: In a three-week postal ballot, a million Americans take part in an exercise to choose the image that will appear on the special Elvis Presley stamp.

18 April 1992: Massachusetts couple Jim and Judith Kelley are married in an Elvis-themed wedding. The top table is decorated by an ice sculpture of Elvis, at each place setting there are Elvis stamp ballots and the entertainment is provided by two Elvis impersonators.

27 April 1992: 'Don't Be Cruel' is played during a fundraising dinner in Boston for Democratic Party presidential hopeful Bill Clinton.

16 May 1992: Nick Caraccio from Queens, New York, better known as 'The King from Queens,' shakes, rattles and rolls during his first television appearance singing 'Blue Suede Shoes' on the USA network, Up All Night.

4 June 1992: Bill Clinton plays 'Heartbreak Hotel' on the saxophone on the Arsenio Hall Show.

An Elvis-themed wedding at the Chapel of Love

4 June 1992: *Anthony Franks, the former US Postmaster-General, reveals on television the result of the stamp ballot. He tells the nation that 277,723 voted for the image of the older Elvis on his special stamp but an overwhelming 851,200 preferred to see Elvis in his youthful prime.*

July 1992: *Yasumasa Mori becomes the first non-American to win the coveted title of the Elvis Presley Impersonation Champion of the World (right).*

21 July 1992: *The Daily Star reports on the outbreak of Elvis wars along a stretch of Streatham High Road in south London. Two restaurants, a mere two doors apart, are both wooing customers with an Elvis impersonator.*

August 1992: *The Caribbean islands of St Vincent and the Grenadines commemorate the fifteenth anniversary of the death of Elvis by issuing a set of nine Elvis Presley stamps.*

12 August 1992: *48 Hours anchorman Dan Rather tells viewers that 44 per cent of all Americans think of themselves as Elvis fans.*

Above: Colonel Tom Parker, Elvis's ex-manager, with the Elvis stamps.

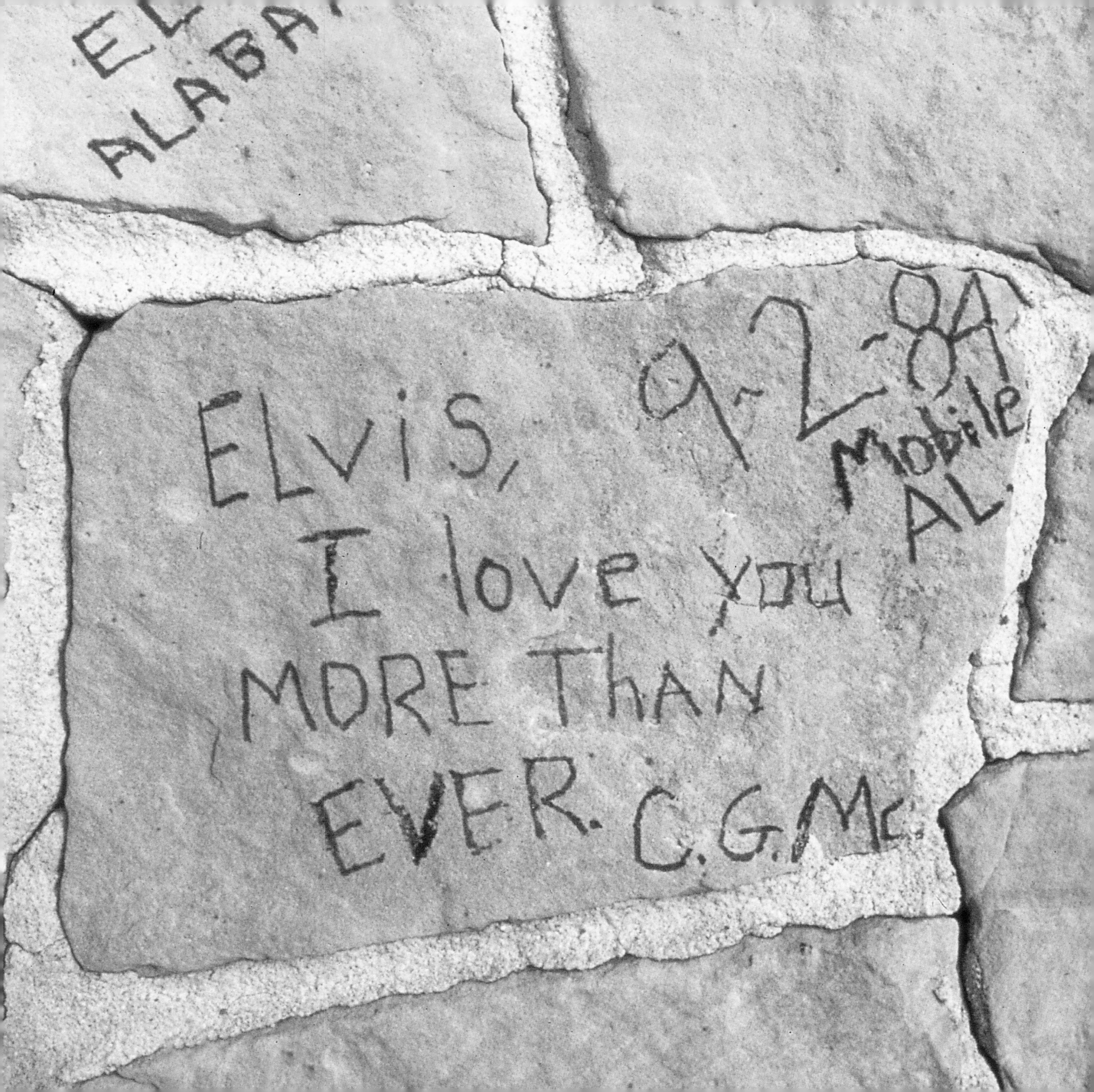
ALABA
9-2-84
Mobile AL
ELVIS,
I love you
MORE THAN
EVER. C.G.Mc

16 August 1992: *More than 25,000 Elvis fans arrive in Memphis and make for Graceland to take part in the annual candlelight vigil which honours Elvis's memory.*

17 August 1992: *The Republican National Convention opens in Texas where 'I saw Elvis at the Republican National Convention in Houston, Texas, August 17 - August 20' badges sell like hot cakes.*

20 August 1992: *The Japanese announce plans to create their own version of Graceland.*

28 August 1992: *The film **Honeymoon in Vegas**, starring Nicolas Cage and James Caan, is released (below) in the US. The movie culminates in a sky-diving display by the thirteen members of the group Flying Elvis.*

24 October 1992: *Elvis's daughter Lisa Marie gives birth to a son, Benjamin Storm.*

19 November 1992: *Elvis is spotted in a square in the Czech capital Prague. Possibly he has come to thank the local radio station Prognosis for playing his music every day.*

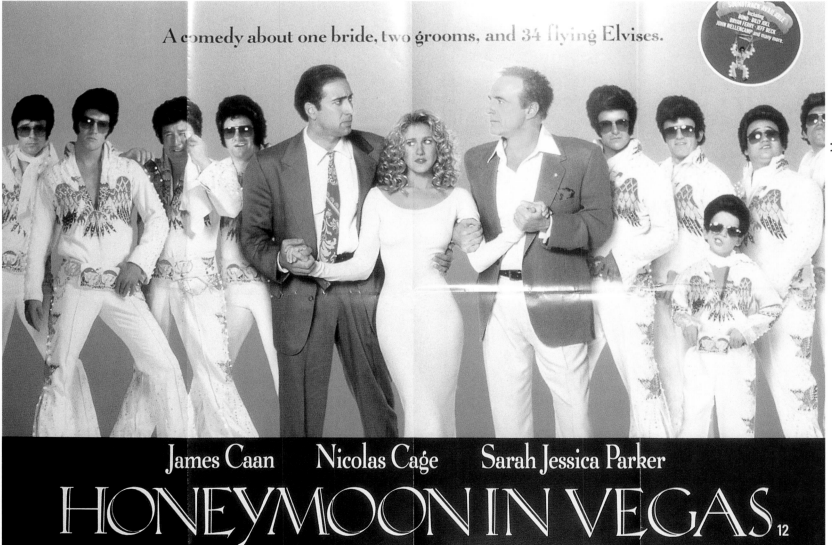

A comedy about one bride, two grooms, and 34 flying Elvises.

James Caan　　Nicolas Cage　　Sarah Jessica Parker

HONEYMOON IN VEGAS 12

20 November 1992: *The RCA boxed set of 140 tracks entitled* **The King of Rock 'n' Roll: the Complete '50s Masters** *reaches platinum in the US and gold elsewhere in the world.*

December 1992: *Amarillo in Texas receives an early batch of the special Elvis stamps by mistake, more than a week before the official launch date.*

1993: *The Official Church of Elvis opens in Portland, Oregon, to a large congregation.*

8 January 1993: *The US postal service issues the Elvis Presley stamp on what would have been his fifty-eighth birthday. The stamp is given an unprecedented initial print run of one million, a figure almost double previous first runs.*

8 January 1993: *Elvis Presley Day is proclaimed in Memphis.*

9 January 1993: *The Richard Nixon Presidential Library sells Nixon/Presley wristwatches for $45 and issues a postcard of the meeting between the two men during Presley's visit to the Oval Office in 1970 (below).*

20 January 1993: *The Boston Globe reports that Elvis tops the list of the Clintons' favourite music and that one of the new President's nicknames is Elvis.*

20 January 1993: *The Boston Globe* reports that Elvis tops the list of the Clintons' favourite music and that one of the new President's nicknames is Elvis.

21 January 1993: It is reported that thousands of Elvis fans are deliberately sending envelopes stamped with the Elvis Presley stamp to addresses which they know to be bogus, so that the mail will come back to them marked 'Return to sender - address unknown'.

1 February 1993: Lisa Marie Presley celebrates her twenty-fifth birthday and so inherits her father's $200 million estate.

17 February 1993: It is announced that Jim Nunn, an unemployed man from Durham, is to be paid £40 a week Enterprise Allowance to work as an Elvis Presley impersonator.

3 May 1993: Andy Warhol's 1963 silkscreen and painting on canvas entitled **Double Elvis** is put up for sale at Sotheby's with an expected price tag of $7-900,000.

14 May 1993: London auction house Christie's sells a 1950s acoustic guitar used by Elvis Presley on **'That's All Right, Mama'** and **'Blue Moon of Kentucky'** for £90,000.

6 July 1993: Restaurateur and Elvis impersonator Paul Elvis Chan is ordered by the authorities in Tunbridge Wells, Kent, to sing a little more softly in his restaurant after complaints from neighbours.

July 1993: Glasgow Elvis impersonator Albert Laing claims that Elvis Presley was in fact Scottish. Among the factors he cites as conclusive evidence is the village of Presley situated in the neighbourhood of Inverness.

31 July 1993: It is reported that Texas rock promoter and producer Bill Smith is suing Graceland for $50,000 because he claims that it spread the false rumour of Elvis's death. He alleges that Presley faked his death and that Graceland had been 'supplementing Elvis Presley's finances ever since.

25 October 1993: *Scotty Moore and D.J. Fontana, two members of Elvis's first band, unveil the plaque decorating a pillar around the information desk at Prestwick airport. This marks the occasion on 2 March 1960 when Elvis made a brief stop-over on his way home from his army service in Germany. It was the only time he set foot on British soil.*

11 November 1993: **The Daily Telegraph** *reports that council workers in Easington, County Durham, have been caught using their short-wave radios to hold Elvis impersonation contests.*

Left: Elvis auction at
Las Vegas, 1994

8 January 1994: *American Airlines offer a cheap round trip to Memphis with a discount of $20 to anybody who turns up at the ticket counter dressed as Elvis Presley.*

8 January 1994: **The Times** *reports that a recent US survey revealed that one American male in thirty-two is an Elvis impersonator.*

13 January 1994: *Writer A.J. Jacobs, author of* **The Two Kings**, *claims that Jesus Christ and Elvis Presley were one and the same man. Among the pieces of evidence he submits, says* **The Sun**, *are the facts that Jesus was baptised in the River Jordan and that Elvis Presley chose the Jordanaires as his backing group.*

18 June 1994: *At the sale of items from the* **Elvis Presley Museum** *held in the* **Las Vegas Hilton**, *actor John Corbett from* **Northern Exposure** *pays more than $60,000 for Elvis's birth certificate and more than $40,000 for his credit card.*

August 1994: *Psychic Kenny Kingston claims that Elvis is 'terribly upset' over Lisa Marie Presley's marriage to Michael Jackson (right). Kingston also reveals that Elvis is studying medicine in the afterlife and that he will return to us in 1997 to practise as a holistic doctor.*

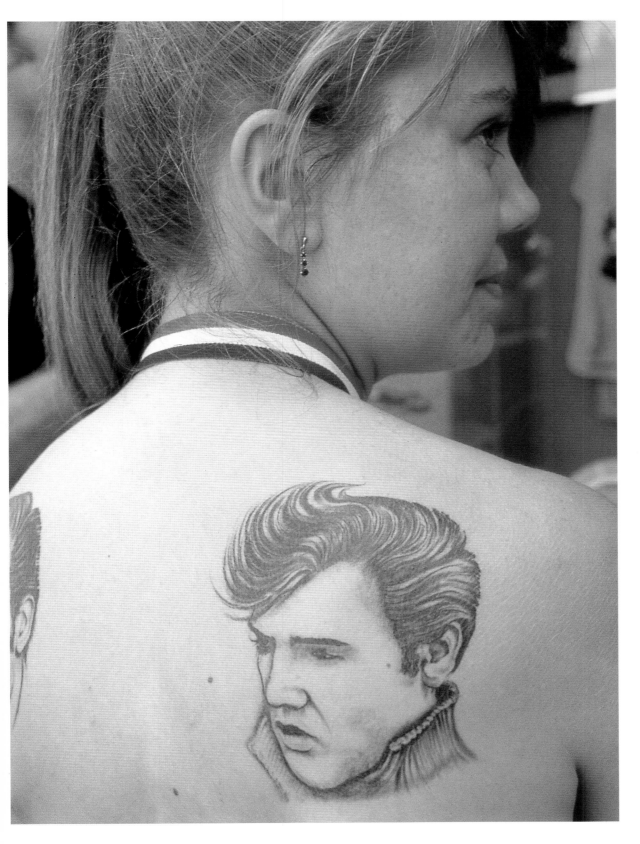

Left: Tattooed Elvis fan.

September 1994: *The Presley Commission issues the Presley Report, which concludes that Elvis is alive and living in a hideout under the federal witness protection scheme.*

September 1994: *There is a reported sighting of Elvis Presley in New York's Yankee Stadium appealing for an end to the baseball players' strike. Could the King have a new role as peacemaker in the world's troublespots?*

5 November 1994: *The **Daily Star** reports that stroke victim Peter Lovesey of Cirencester in Gloucestershire has recovered his power of speech while singing '**Love Me Tender**' at a karaoke night in his local pub.*

21 November 1994: *According to the **Daily Telegraph**, the Flying Elvis, one group of Elvis impersonators, is suing the Flying Elvises, a rival troupe, in Las Vegas over the question of who has the right to parachute from an aeroplane wearing rhinestone suits while miming to Elvis songs.*

24 November 1994: *The **Sun** reveals that Eunice Fitch of Cannock, Staffordshire, suffering from a brain tumour, has* *awakened from a coma after seeing a vision of Elvis Presley.*

1995: *The University of Memphis establishes a $25,000 scholarship endowment fund for music and drama students on behalf of the Elvis Presley Memorial Foundation Inc.*

8 January 1995: *On what would have been his sixtieth birthday Elvis Presley is featured on the front cover of* **Life** *magazine (opposite).*

8 January 1995: *QVC, the Home Shopping Channel, presents a special Elvis Presley birthday show.*

8 January 1995: *South London woman Shirley Fitzgerald times the arrival of her third son Rhys to coincide with the birthday of her idol Elvis Presley.*

12 February 1995: *Elvis impersonator Brian Lee takes the bold step of sinking his life savings into hiring the London Palladium for the night. He does his act before an audience which eventually reaches fifteen hundred.*

1 March 1995: **The Guardian** *reports that Finnish academic Jukka Ammondt will produce a CD of Elvis Presley songs translated into Latin. The disc will include such favourites as* **'Tenere Me Ama'** *(***'Love Me Tender'***) and* **'Nunc Hic Aut Numquam'** *(***'It's Now or Never'***).*

12 March 1995: *The Graceland kitchen is opened to the public.*

9 April 1995: *According to the* **Sunday Express***, Rolling Stone Mick Jagger has bought the film rights to* **'Last Train to Memphis'** *by Peter Guralnik. Will Mick play the King?*

May/June 1995: *Pastor Mort Frandu opens the First Presleyterian Church of Elvis the Divine in Denver, complete with a set of thirty-one commandments for the faithful to follow.*

21 July 1995: *George Nichopoulous, a.k.a. Elvis's medical man Dr Nick, is struck off the register for prescription irregularities.*

6 August 1995: *Oxford, Mississippi, hosts the first University of Mississippi Annual Elvis Presley Conference.*

26 August 1995: *Bad Neuheim in Germany unveils a pillar with the effigy of Elvis and his guitar to mark his military service in the area.*

31 August 1995: *Not to be outdone, rival town Friedberg names a square after Elvis Presley and hosts a three-day US Army celebration.*

2 April 1996: **Elvis** *by Ray Cooney and Jack Good is revived at London's Prince of Wales Theatre with Alexander Bar as the boy Elvis and Tim Whitnall and P.J. Proby returning to the show in which they starred at its premiere in 1977.*

COLLECTOR'S EDITION

LIFE

ON
HIS
60TH
BIRTHDAY:
A
CELEBRATION
IN
PICTURES

WINTER 1995

COUNTRY	PRICE	COUNTRY	PRICE
Austria	S 60	Italy	Lir 6,500
Belgium	F 190	Luxembourg	LUF 190
Denmark	Kr 30	Netherlands	Fl 8.50
Finland	MK 22	Norway	Kr 29
France	F 29	Portugal Cont.	Esc 650
Germany	DM 9	Spain	Pta 590
Greece	Dr 850	Sweden	Kr 30
Ireland	IR £2.70 (incl. tax)	Switzerland	SFr 7.00
		U.K.	£2.50

9 770024 301995

135

Illustrations

Elvis Spins a Disc, 1983

Special photography by Angelo Hornak.